Residential Care for Children

A Review of the Research

Residential Care
for Children

A Review of the Research

by

Roger Bullock

Michael Little

Spencer Millham

Dartington Social Research Unit

London: HMSO

ISBN 0 11 321590 8

Designed and produced by Kevin Mount
of the Dartington Social Research Unit
Typesetting in Monotype® Bembo, Sabon and
Gill Sans by Icon Graphic Services, Exeter

Contents

Introduction

The last two decades have seen a rapid decline in the use of residential care for children. The movement has been most noticeable in the public sector, that is, for children cared for by health and social services, but the trend is a general one, equally apparent in the boarding schools and the armed forces. A similar pattern is commonly discernible elsewhere in the Western world.

This review examines research into residential child-care undertaken since the Second World War. Most of the studies cited are British or North American but relevant work from other countries, such as Israel, has been included. Because funders and investigators cannot be even-handed in selecting aspects of residence for scrutiny, findings are not uniformly authoritative. Thus, this study not only focuses on what is known, but draws attention to gaps in our knowledge.

Any review of the research is to a degree a review of the service. Residential child-care dominated statutory and voluntary services for many years, giving rise to an extensive literature on its merits and deficiencies. In the immediate post-war period, fuelled by the anxieties generated by the separation experiences of wartime, the principal concern was to discover whether children long in residential care might become institutionalised. Later, as treatment programmes were introduced, the central question became, "does residence make any difference?". More recently, in the light of better understanding, residence has become established as merely one facet of a larger package of interventions available to social workers. The changing role of residential care is apparent in the topics that have interested researchers.

Our scrutiny may go some way towards satisfying the demands of commentators who complain that there exists no coherent theory capable of informing decisions on the subject of residential care. They argue that it is necessary to know why residential care is unique and why it is to be preferred in certain circumstances. In fact, several such theoretical approaches are suggested by research since 1945 and they are collected at the end of this introductory essay.

Such are our aims. As for the practicalities of reviewing research, our first task was to decide what we should take the term research to mean. Many influential texts on residential care have not been research in the pure scientific sense but official reports, such as *Curtis, Wagner* and *Utting,* or inquiries following scandals, such as the Carlton riot in 1959 or that into the use of 'pindown' in Staffordshire. Other studies record the insights and pronouncements of clinicians, such as Bettelheim or Docker-Drysdale. These are different in kind from research that assesses evidence in the light of competing theories.

In order to be comprehensive, we have considered all research on institutional settings (including investigations that many might disregard) which has made some impact on services for children in local authority care. For example, in view of the light it sheds on the predicament of deprived children, we refer to the extensive literature on children's experiences of hospital and boarding in the independent schools. Indeed, different approaches to the subject of residence have tended to inform one another.

Because more that 100 studies seem to us to be relevant, we have separated them into groups representing work undertaken before and after 1975. That year has been chosen as the dividing line because it saw the publication of *Varieties of Residential Experience,* which brought together a number of papers based on studies in the 1960s and early 1970s. The date is given further significance by the fact that when *Varieties of Residential Experience* was published, only 4 of the 14 researchers whose work was included were still active in the residential field. Parallels can be drawn between the British experience and that of North America and Israel which also had a strong tradition in the area in the 1960s but saw research after 1975 becoming less sustained.

If the focus of attention is restricted to empirical studies of residential child-care and education, 26 were completed before 1975 and 35 thereafter. They include most of the major published work, but, for brevity, some relevant articles that have appeared in academic journals have been omitted. Reference is also made to another 56 texts influential in the process of planning residential services.

Each study is explored in relation to various aspects of residential care. The categories cover the history of care services, the characteristics of entrants, the reasons for admission, the routes of entry taken by clients, the goals and regimes of the institutions, as well as influential factors such as the informal cultures of staff and children. A complete list is included in the three summary Diagrams included in the Directory, which forms the second part of this publication.

Research before 1975

The study of residential care before 1960 seems to have been undertaken chiefly with the aim of informing some wider social or psychological theory. Bowlby, for example, studied 44 juvenile thieves while developing his views on attachment and separation. One of the first British investigations of residence as a social system in its own right was Townsend's investigation of old people's homes, part of a wider programme of research into the condition of the elderly in society.

In the 1960s, for a variety of reasons, research interest shifted from theoretical perspectives to the institutions themselves, gaining impetus, paradoxically, from theoretical dissertations rather than empirical evidence. In 1961, the American author Goffman published *Asylums,* which elaborated the influential concept of totality. A year later came Polsky's *Cottage Six* which illuminated the inner world of residential settings. At the same time, in Britain, Barton was highlighting the apathy and dependence exhibited by institutionalised patients in mental hospitals. Organisational theory was also beginning to suggest links between the various components of institutions, indicating connections between residents' behaviour and the quality of regimes.

Thus, the interest in research into residential care for children took root and several groups in Britain developed theoretical perspectives and suggested ways in which institutions might be explored. In our pre-Dartington days at the King's College Research Centre in Cambridge, we published *A Manual to the Sociology of the School* which offered a conceptual framework and a methodology for understanding boarding schools. At the Thomas Coram Research Unit and the Maudsley Hospital, Bartak, King, Rutter, Raynes and the Tizards devised methodologies for comparing and evaluating different residential approaches. The Home Office Research Unit, too, made pioneering studies of the effects of different regimes, good examples of which are Dunlop's work on approved schools, Heal and Cawson's analysis of institutional climates and Sinclair's comparative study of probation hostels. In addition, two experimental modifications of regimes were evaluated: Cornish and Clarke conducted a controlled trial in which approved school boys deemed suitable for therapeutic care were randomly allocated to contrasting regimes; Bottoms and McClintock at the Cambridge Institute of Criminology meticulously traced changes in regime at Dover Borstal.

The academic debate engendered by this flurry of research activity was reviewed in *Varieties of Residential Experience*. For example, Clarke and Martin of the Home Office Research Unit argued that absconding from reform schools was predominantly learned behaviour; at Dartington we preferred an interactionist approach, stressing the significance of environmental factors. Sinclair, on the other hand, attempted to reconcile opposing positions. The argument was enlivened by the interest of researchers in other countries, who were engaged in investigating similar problems in a variety of residential schools, treatment units and homes.

In the immediate post-war years, there was firm belief in residential care as a treatment approach. Its proponents were convinced that scientific research would provide a solution to children's problems and that the institutions themselves would be able to carry out these successful treatments. Such confidence is evident in the Government's *Care and Treatment in a Planned Environment* (1970) known to staff in the reformatory as the 'yellow peril', as much for its radical message as the colour of its cover. Debate so fundamental is noticeably absent from the literature on current British residential child-care. In this context, it is interesting that absconding should have ceased to interest researchers once the approved schools moved into the child-care system and became CHEs (Community Homes with Education) in 1974. As a result, running away was no longer an administrative problem, yet absconding remains an issue that greatly affects the welfare of children in care.

The focus before 1975

An examination of the studies undertaken prior to 1975 shows that certain aspects of the subject received greater attention than others. Facilities for children with physical and mental disabilities and for the seriously delinquent were given copious coverage. On the other hand, ordinary residential homes in England and Wales, which in 1971 sheltered over 30,000 children, were virtually ignored.

As much is immediately apparent from Diagram A (Page30), which summarises the research undertaken before 1975. It can be seen that most residential studies of the period concentrated on long stays; the use of residential facilities for acute and brief placements was rarely considered. Most of the evidence is derived from studies of approved schools and other provision for difficult adolescents, such as special boarding schools;

children's homes and penal establishments receive little attention. It is also evident that the focus was on organisational goals, regimes and structures and on staff and residents' adaptations; less notice was taken of the historical antecedents of services or of the routes or avenues young people took before entering residential care. What we now call consumer studies were virtually unknown.

In short, before 1975, residential approaches tended to be viewed by researchers as isolated interventions, a perspective in tune with the treatment and client focus fashionable at the time. There is little interest in the role of establishments in wider welfare systems. Similarly, outcome evidence is uncommon and, when available, is usually restricted to reconviction rates for offenders. Other aspects of residential life, such as relations between the institutions and the children's families or between the organisation and the outside world, were neglected.

Main findings of the research

The foregoing reservations apart, there is much valuable information to be gleaned from the research of the period; indeed, many of earlier researchers' conclusions are supported by more recent work. However, many of the issues that seemed salient before 1975 are no longer relevant. For example, reform in juvenile justice means that most boys and girls then in reformatory schools would not even be in state care today, let alone in residential settings. Similarly, certain goals of researchers seem rather optimistic twenty years on, such as the quest for the cause of delinquency or the dream of a universally effective regime. Nevertheless, many of the conclusions arrived at are valuable and relevant. They can be summarised as follows:

Institutional goals

Generally, the more child-centred and overtly caring the regime, the better the outcome for children, from the point of view of their education, personal growth, development and social conduct.

Residential regimes

It emerges from the studies of absconding and violence that different residential regimes produce markedly different responses among staff and children and so affect the behaviour of young people while they are in the institution.

Formal structures

How well institutions function is more important than the characteristics of their administrative structure. For example, consensus among staff about the proper approach to child-care is vital; it matters less whether such agreement is reached by charismatic leadership, egalitarian team-work or good staff communications.

Effects and outcomes

The informal cultures created by staff and children are especially significant in influencing performance. In successful institutions, they reinforce child-care aims; in poor quality establishments, the presence of hostile cultures can seriously undermine effectiveness.

The impact of a residential experience on the behaviour of young people is less discernible after they have left. However, this is a finding based largely on studies of persistent property offenders for whom the prognosis is poor whatever form intervention takes.

Good residential care can provide children with a stable home and a stimulating educational environment. It can widen their cultural horizons and create a framework for emotionally secure relationships with adults. It can also provide a basis for more intensive therapeutic work. The weaknesses of residential settings lie in their inability to give unconditional love, the constraints they place on a child's emotional development, their inability to ensure staff continuity and the peripheral role they allocate to children's families.

Residential institutions emerge as complex organisations impossible to classify on the basis of simple criteria. For example, a liberal, formal regime may accompany a strong, intolerant inmate culture. Similarly, depending on the susceptibilities of the individual, expressive sanctions, such as moral opprobrium or adult disapproval, may be as painful as the loss of liberty. Rarely can institutions be assessed according to clear continua, such as might connect the liberal at one extreme to the repressive at the other, or a 'group' as opposed to an 'individual' orientation.

When looking at more than one institution therefore, researchers must be certain they are comparing like with like. The most fruitful of pre-1975 investigations looked beyond the stated aims and functions and considered their style and ethos: whether the residential approaches were academic or vocational, how the informal societies of staff and children related to each other and to the formal system. Understanding the nature of residential care resulted from an exploration of several avenues, not one in isolation.

Nevertheless, although a variety of institutions was scrutinised, there was little exploration of the relationship between residential care and child-care services generally. Residential care was considered generally ineffective, but so little was known of outcomes in other areas of child-care that accurate assessments could not be made – a lack of knowledge that had serious policy implications.

Research since 1975

Research undertaken since 1975 reflects a changing view of child-care services. Naturally, much research concentrated on areas previously neglected, but an important change also took place in ideas. Belief in the value of treatment significantly declined, partly as a result of changing ideological fashion (treatment was seen as unethical and intrusive by liberals and as expensive and ineffective by traditionalists), partly because the results of certain residential experiments, particularly with delinquents, were proving disappointing. The focus of reform in juvenile delinquency thus shifted from the manipulation of institutional regimes to the provision of alternatives in the community: children were to be kept at home whenever possible and specialist fostering schemes developed for the most difficult.

It can be seen from the summary Diagram B (Page 10) that research since 1975 has been patchy. Indeed very few studies of residential services in their own right have been undertaken and many findings in the field have been merely incidental to research into other areas. For example, the longitudinal data gathered by Quinton and Rutter, by ourselves and by Rowe and her colleagues, as well as by Fanshel and Shinn in New York State, provided much new evidence concerning the use and effects of residential care but far less on the interventions themselves. This is hardly surprising since Quinton and Rutter's main interest was in intergenerational continuities of behaviour while the other three were primarily studies of placement patterns and sequences. This research has certainly filled gaps in our knowledge, such as the role of residential care in the wider welfare system and the avenues along which children pass before admission to care, but other areas remain neglected.

Gaps left by recent research cannot be filled by knowledge gained from the pre-1975 studies, because residential establishments have changed so much since the 1960s. Statistics for England and Wales reveal a sharp fall in the number of children in residential placements, from 60,000 in 1970 to 13,000 in 1990, and at the same time show an increase in the average age of the children sheltered. Older adolescents and young adults present different problems from younger children, and the former should not be viewed simply as the latter writ large. Similarly, it seems likely that young people now placed in residential care are increasingly those with serious problems – more so than was the case for earlier generations, otherwise they would be supported at home or fostered.

Individual children are probably no more difficult, although the greater awareness of child abuse has complicated matters, but institutional populations now comprise an increasing proportion of disturbed and damaged individuals. This poses new control problems for staff who may resort to unacceptable practices. The group dynamics in residential care today simply do not mirror those of thirty years ago. Paradoxically, before 1975, when the majority of residents were young and relatively harmless, the research emphasis was on older delinquents. Since 1975, when the majority of residents are older and less benign, such research as there has been has concentrated on younger children.

Gaps in the focus since 1975

Diagram B, which summarises the research since 1975, indicates several neglected areas, the chief of which is short-stay residential care. Only follow-up studies have shed light on this intervention. Our study of separated children, *Lost in Care*, for example, reveals that over 40% of the short-stay cases had a residential placement. Rowe and her colleagues went on to show that the circumstances in which it was relied upon were very wide ranging. It provides a place of refuge in an emergency and contributes to more complex tasks of assessment, preparation for fostering and independence, and sheltering those remanded by the courts. Indeed, a child's four week sojourn in an observation and assessment centre can serve many purposes other than assessment. They include control, gatekeeping access to expensive resources and containing delinquency. Yet, in spite of its widespread use, very little is known about the nature and effects of short-stay residential care.

Available research offers little in the way of quality assessment. Even in an area as contentious as secure accommodation, where several studies have been undertaken, there is little information on the quality of the care offered to the children. It is a serious omission. To discover what use is made of a service without considering the quality of life it provides or even the methods it employs can have unsatisfactory consequences. Some of the studies cited include some form of outcome assessment of residents, but in their scope they usually fall well short of the criteria laid out in Parker and colleagues' recent publication, *Looking After Children: Assessing Outcomes in Child-Care*. An attempt to meet the standards laid down in the 1989 *Children Act* is being made through careful application of these outcome measures and the criteria for inspection and quality control laid out in the guidance and regulations.

Not only has research failed to focus on short-stay residential care or the quality of the care offered, it has signally failed to address the subject of the degree to which sectors of child-care services overlap. The dearth of information on the subject suggests that it may well be a most fruitful area for study. For example, studies of young people in secure units have uncovered a relationship between the populations of young offenders' institutions and child-care units, and recent research in Warwickshire has considered the effect of the closure of children's homes on entries to special education. More exploration of this ground is needed.

The same may well be said of long-term outcomes of young people who have experienced residential interventions. The general conclusions reached by Quinton and Rutter and Triseliotis and Russell are still likely to be relevant, but it must be remembered that their results are based on services in the 1960s. If we are to assess the value of residential interventions in the 1990s, we must have more recent research related to current practice on which to base our conclusions.

Diagram B highlights certain residential settings that have received scant attention in recent years. The welfare aspects of special (EBD) boarding schools, in which over 1,000 children a year are placed by social services, remain unexplored. The ordinary boarding schools continue to escape examination, despite the fact that they have experienced significant changes in their populations and regimes and shelter the largest residential population of any sector, probably as many as 150,000 children. Affluence does not necessarily extinguish need. We simply do not know what children looked after in such schools require, let alone whether their needs are being met.

Other studies of direct relevance to the work of child-care authorities would focus on young people in remand centres and young offenders' institutions. Work with these groups is badly needed because under the 1991 *Criminal Justice Act* responsibility for some adolescents has passed from the Home Office to social services departments. The older adolescent offender poses special problems for the residential sector and may cause local authorities to reconsider policies and plans for the young people they look after.

Finally, although statistics show a reduction in residential populations, the number of children living in voluntary homes, hostels and other accommodation, much of which may be residential, continues to be probably over 2,000. It is not clear from existing research what children sheltered in these settings require, what such placements offer or whether their quality is satisfactory. Yet, given the distinction increasingly made between case responsibility and case management, this amorphous group is likely to remain significant.

Lack of interest in what happens inside residential institutions and in the quality of child-care is reflected in two other features of Diagram B. By comparison with the pre-1975 research, there is little on regimes or the relationships between the institution and the outside world, in particular with regard to children's families and social networks. Recent studies have partially addressed such concerns, but a fuller assessment is needed if the 1989 *Children Act* is to be properly implemented. The rights of parents whose children are looked after away from home also need to be respected.

A major contribution of recent research has been to improve understanding of the functions of residential care for the wider child-care system, but it has lacked careful analysis of children's background characteristics and needs. Much more sophisticated data will have to be obtained if we are to gain a full understanding of the contribution that residential care can make to the services of the 1990s.

Comparative studies are of enormous value, and criteria by which accurate comparisons can be made between cases receiving different interventions are an essential requirement. Yet comparative research is rare, even between different types of interventions. For example, only Colton has attempted systematically to compare residential and foster care.

Because there is so little information on children's backgrounds, it has been very difficult to appreciate the scale of change in clientele that has taken place in community homes over the years. The findings of *Children in the Public Care* concerning the age, gender and ethnic composition of homes appear to have been regarded with surprise, but these data are essential if services are to be monitored and elaborate research undertaken. With better information, it would be possible to link children's needs with institutional approaches and draw attention to significant changes in key features of peer groups, an area already highlighted as particularly important.

The Diagrams show what research is available, but an extensive entry does not necessarily imply comprehensive or authoritative knowledge. For example, despite having data on children's family backgrounds and presenting problems, we know little about their health. The special needs of particular groups, including girls and certain ethnic minorities, are not sufficiently understood. The management of minorities within a diverse population has rarely been considered and studies of informal staff and child worlds in institutions have tended to be very general. Hence the anxieties of workers, who must try to reconcile the demands of management with the needs of those for whom they care, have not been properly considered. Similarly, concepts such as the identity, personal growth and development of children and the values and intellectual development of staff require greater scrutiny. Indeed, in the light of recent events in Staffordshire and Leicestershire, there is a pressing need to examine the source of staff expertise and the forces that shape staff morale and ideologies.

Certain areas are almost entirely unexplored. Residential establishments are brimming with older teenagers, but hardly anything has been written about the sexual behaviour of young people. The possibility of sexual attraction between young staff and older teenage residents is scarcely acknowledged and the homosexuality of staff or residents is still a taboo subject. Little research has been done into the spiritual and expressive needs of children. As for the much talked about but seldom studied subject of the appropriateness of residential care for victims of child abuse, there is not sufficient evidence to make an informed decision. Indeed, it is possible that children face some risk of being further abused while in residential care. Certainly society's awareness of child abuse has sometimes led to a wholly regrettable, strained and artificial relationship betwen staff and children, engendered by staff fears of abuse accusations.

Findings of the research

The preceding reservations apart, recent research has added much to our knowledge. In particular it has increased awareness of:

Resident populations and their needs
Children placed in residential care are likely to be older adolescents, many of whom will present special difficulties or be *in extremis*. The populations

of residential units will be varied and a range of needs and presenting problems has to be met. Many children say they prefer residential care to fostering because it is less restrictive and minimises conflict with family loyalties, so preserving trust and confidence. However, there is a high risk of a poor outcome, and it may therefore be of limited value. The views of the children are important and the 1989 *Children Act* stresses the need to respect their wishes, but their preferences may spring from insecurity and isolation more than understanding of their long-term best interests.

Routes children take

The sequence of decisions and placements that leads to admission to residential care is well-established. At certain points along the way, social work decisions may well aggravate a child's problems, for example by placing a run-away in a setting with a high absconding rate, or far from home. Concern about the risks inherent in social work procedure has generated much research interest in the consequences for a child's care career of a particular sequence of placement decisions.

Functions for the wider child-care system

Follow-up studies of children in care show that residence is used more frequently than commonly thought. Four-fifths of children long separated have a taste of residential care. Also, residential care can intervene at different points in a child's care career, such as on entry to care or subsequent to a foster home breakdown. Frequently it is not the only intervention: nearly one-third of long-stay cases experience both foster and residential care.

Effects and outcomes while in residence

Admission to residential care creates secondary problems associated with stigma, separation and strained relationships within the institution. These can so preoccupy the child and his or her carers that the primary problems necessitating removal from home are neglected. In the context of a child's wider care career, the residential experience may be of only marginal relevance; major effects on behaviour are seldom to be expected. Indeed, the problems separated children experience as they try to preserve the continuity of their personal and family relationships may overwhelm any benefit that might reasonably be expected to accrue.

Effects and outcomes on leaving residence

Unless they are persistent offenders, children leaving residential care face problems markedly different from those that necessitated entry. Impetuous and difficult behaviour has usually declined, but now unemployment, isolation and homelessness loom.

Long-term effects and outcomes

The research suggests that residential care confers educational benefits and offers children stability in an otherwise disrupted life. Certain psychological gains can also be made and useful social skills acquired. Some beneficial change may, of course, result from the maturation process. Indeed, a major contribution of residential care may simply lie in its capacity to accommodate children, thus offering them an environment for their growing up.

It should be borne in mind that the strengths and weaknesses of residential care may not always be apparent from studies of young people while resident. For example, follow-up research suggests that some children who are difficult and very unsettled while there do quite well in the longer term – some girls for example - while others, such as withdrawn and institutionalised boys, generally fare badly and drift into homelessness and recidivism. The subsequent behaviour of persistent property offenders is also rarely altered by placement in a residential setting.

A problem inherent in discussions about recent research has been the tendency to confuse the shortcomings of residential care with those of state care generally. In other contexts, such as in elite or higher education, research excites far less criticism. We need to differentiate the categories of care placements more carefully in research evaluations, so that the different nature and quality of inputs can be compared. We also need to study the combinations and sequences of interventions likely to be employed under the 1989 *Children Act*, in order to assess care approaches more accurately. An analysis of the different dimensions of key factors, such as the different meanings children and administrators attribute to the size of groups, also needs to be undertaken. Finally, a sharper distinction needs to be drawn between studies of children in residential care, which suggests a process perspective, and residential care as a service, which implies more of a systems approach.

Theories of residential care

If residential care is to succeed in improving the quality of young people's lives, providers and clients need to be aware of what good research indicates are its strengths and weaknesses. Just what is the theoretical basis for residential services, and how can it be used to underpin what the state provides?

The primary purpose of a theory is to explain, which in social research usually involves identifying causal links between situations and between the investment of resources and its results. Thus we might predict how responses and outcomes from residence will vary with different levels of institutional totality. Theories can also illuminate and clarify the issue under scrutiny. A theory, such as that of adolescent independence, may be general and simply part of the panoply of ideas concerning child development, or it may be specific to a set of circumstances, such as the hypothesis that as young people move towards adulthood, emotional support from the family endures long after institutional support has ceased.

Because it is used to promote children's welfare in society's name, residential child-care must be based on tested theory: profound commitment and conviction cannot be relied upon. However, in an area of human affairs so complex, no single comprehensive theory is possible: many different perspectives are relevant and should be considered complementary.

Certain institutional processes are best understood in terms of organisational theory which stresses the need for fundamental agreement between the constituent parts of an institution. For example, staff roles should not conflict and hostile resident cultures should be controlled. Etzioni suggests that effective and tranquil institutions demonstrate *compliance* between aims, resident and staff roles, and the controls employed. A number of theories of child development are also relevant, ranging from those of Freud and Jung, through Piaget, to those expounded by Winnicott and Bowlby. Thirdly, the legislation enshrines principles which are themselves based on theories as to what constitutes effective care. For example, the 1989 *Children Act* encourages shared care, redefines parental responsibility and, with its emphasis on services to all 'children in need', marks a departure from 'child rescue' philosophies of earlier decades. Finally, there are theories relating to specific residential interventions: how the needs of children are tackled and why one approach is more effective than another.

Several other theories might be investigated, such as group dynamics or educational development, but the four highlighted here are sufficient to demonstrate that within any residential institution, recognition of a number of theories is implicit. For a residential service to be effective, it is necessary to ensure that the theories embraced by an institution are appropriate to the conditions and to minimise conflict between competing theories. It is not much use a well organised residential home delivering an irrelevant service, but integrating theories in a residential setting can be difficult. Effectiveness in one area of children's lives, such as behaviour therapy, may be at the expense of success elsewhere, such as personal growth and development. The task is to maximise the gains and minimise losses, to use Whitaker's phrase.

Theories change, pass out of fashion or are discredited by argument and research. We balk at eugenics, reject Burt's categories of intellectual retardation and apply versions of Freud and Piaget much changed from the original. Theory also reflects the age in which it flourishes. When the great institutions of the 19th century were built, their fabric rested on the foundations of apparently sound, frequently radical ideas. The mental hospitals offered asylum in which treatment and therapies could be applied free from the contaminating influence of the outside world. Likewise, the reform schools and borstals were established to protect the young offender from unhelpful adult influences, to provide by example alternatives to a life of crime and to train lads in 'appropriate' vocational skills. Such approaches were reasonable and frequently quite successful responses to contemporary problems. But social contexts change, a new generation presents new problems and a residential institution, often inward-looking and entangled by redundant ideologies, becomes increasingly vulnerable. Some, such as the English public schools, adapt rapidly and stay in business; others, such as the self-styled progressive schools, whose educational philosophies were so influential in the mid–20th century, decay.

The value of residential care lies in the breadth of the approach. The rise in the number of children sheltered in large institutions in the 19th century can be explained, at least in part, by a desire to offer children a total experience encompassing every aspect of their life and capable of enhancing their spiritual well-being as well as their physical and psychological health. Indeed, it was the need to shelter children from religious schism and change that led to the rapid rise in boarding school provision in 19th century England.

In the United Kingdom and elsewhere decline characterises the use of residential settings for a wide range of clients. Children can be educated just as well in day schools; moral and spiritual matters seem to concern us less; health problems have been much diminished by better preventative medicine. Demand for a total experience may nevertheless still exist, for example in response to health and other problems of special need or among minorities that attach high priority to religious upbringing. In addition, emphasis on the value of a total experience which protects the child from external damaging influences survives in the psycho-therapeutic child-care tradition

Critics of residential care argue that a total experience within the walls of a residential institution damages children's development. It may be true in some contexts, but in others institutionalisation is esteemed. For example, characteristics valued by the middle classes, such as self-control and the concealment of emotion, are best learned during the long process of socialisation provided by elite boarding schools and universities. So one should not be too hasty in discounting the ideas which supported the expansion of the residential sector nor unquestioningly accept the arguments used to explain its decline. Indeed, it is puzzling why societies such as those in the Islamic tradition have not adopted residential solutions to social problems.

We raise these theories to show how they can be of value in understanding residential services. Moreover, we would propose that an effective residential centre would develop an approach which integrated several of them. For example, in long-stay treatment units catering for very difficult adolescents a number of ideas are combined and reflected in the day-to-day care of the residents. A clearly stated treatment policy reflects well thought out theories of child development and behaviour, such as the cause of psychological disorder and the possibility of improvement in different pathologies. The organisation of the units is also consistent with these theoretical approaches. Entry is closely guarded and, once the young person has been admitted, the treatment programme reflects his or her development. This general approach is supported by legislation which protects the child's rights and ensures that long stays in restrictive settings are avoided wherever possible.

Gaps in our knowledge

Because of the present level of public and professional concern about residential care, there are good grounds for hoping that there will be new research to remedy the gaps in knowledge indicated in this discussion. Our review suggests the following relevant areas:

The effects of the 1989 Children Act

Several new areas introduced by the 1989 *Children Act* will benefit from monitoring and evaluation. The procedural implications for residential care of certain concepts and principles defined by the Act, namely, significant harm, beyond parental control and children in need are considerable, since each has implications for referral patterns, regimes and decision-making. In addition, attention needs to be paid to changes in ethos and practice arising from the legislation. Key in this respect will be a monitoring of the use and interpretation of Volume 4 of the *Children Act* regulations, the operation and effect of the new registration and inspection requirements and the ways in which complaints procedures are used by children and families. The management of voluntary arrangements to look after children and the inclusive nature of social work decision-making are also important issues raised by the introduction of the new legislation.

Research into particular types of residence

It is useful to distinguish between research into residential institutions and studies which focus upon particular groups of children. In the former, three categories of provision deserve greater scrutiny. These are ordinary boarding schools sheltering children looked after by social services departments, special boarding schools, and residential provision for the older adolescents, particularly hostels and dormitory provision offered to the young single homeless.

Research into specific groups of children

Within any general research strategy, particular groups of vulnerable children can become neglected. Particularly ill served in past research into residential care have been girls, abuse victims and short-stay cases. Because social workers employ residential care for children who find it difficult to settle in alternative family situations, we also need to understand what happens when children from diverse backgrounds and with different needs are thrust together. The composition of the residential group is an important factor in the individual care plans required by the 1989 *Children Act*.

Questions that deserve fresh scrutiny

Yesterday's questions are not the ones we would pose today. For example, although Berridge's study of the smaller children's home well describes the situation in 1984, change in this area has been considerable and more knowledge is needed. Similarly, the 1989 *Children Act* and the 1991 *Criminal Justice Act* suggest the need for further exploration of the circumstances of young offenders remanded to security, sentenced to youth custody or experiencing a community placement as an alternative to residential care.

There is much to be said for re-scrutiny of regimes and styles of residential approach, particularly for a comparison between child-care, education and health settings for children. Finally in this area, there is scope for a wider analysis of the various outcomes of the residential experience. The focus of earlier studies has tended to be offending behaviour as an outcome, but several recent studies have used a range of criteria for assessing children's development and evaluating their life chances. Such approaches should be extended.

New dimensions of the residential experience

Certain spiritual and expressive needs of children have been overlooked. Too little is known about the extent to which interests, such as those connected with art, music, literature and popular culture, are recognised and developed in residential settings. Central to the pursuit of these objectives is what residential social workers are actually able to achieve, which in turn raises thorny issues of social work training and the barriers, formal and informal, to good practice in caring for children.

A study of the organisation of residential homes and schools would also be informative. An important focus would be the relationship between residential institutions and outside agencies, children's families, friends and schools. Relations with senior managers and advisers within the organisation responsible for running the home and external agencies which share responsibility for the child are also important, because the 1989 *Children Act* is likely to increase inter-departmental sponsorship of children.

Finally, a new evaluation of the ideas, theories and treatments which underpin various forms of residential provision would benefit from recent methodological innovation. It is over 30 years since the systematic studies of treatment pioneered by Cornish and Clarke at Kingswood and by Bottoms and McClintock at Dover Borstal were undertaken. Today we are less certain about what residential social workers seek to provide and less clear still about what difference their contribution makes to the lives of the children in their care. The issues could well be explored through an evaluation of outcomes based upon random allocation of children to different approaches, centres or regimes. This might be feasible if allocation were to take place within broad bands of options all of which were considered to be in the best interests of the child. An alternative would be to consider the outcome of different combinations of intervention. It is now possible to compare the effects of one residential placement with those produced by a combination of residential care, fostering and placements at home or with relatives.

Conclusions

This completes our review of the research literature on residential child-care. It has sought to summarise the main approaches adopted over many years and attempted to give general findings. This has not been an easy task and we have found it useful to distinguish studies conducted before 1975 from those of more recent origin. Also, we have referred to several general texts on residential child-care which, although not empirical studies in their own right, are based on research. Finally, we have sought to demonstrate the need for theoretical dimensions to residential care and have identified research gaps which we believe need to be filled. Residential child-care is a complex, slow and expensive business and change cannot be introduced quickly. A sound research and development programme, while not making things easier, may at least ensure that change follows the right lines.

In the Directory that follows, studies relevant to particular aspects of residential care are listed. This makes it possible to identify those areas that have received most research attention. Diagram A summarises studies prior to 1975, Diagram B summarises studies completed since 1975 and Diagram C indicates the general and theoretical books on residential care. Each text has been given a reference number; more detail on each study can be found by using this number as a key to the index that follows each Diagram.

Part Two
Directory of Publications

A

Publications before 1975

Publications before 1975

Numbers refer to the alphabetical listings on pages 32-39

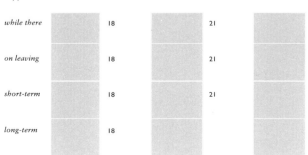

Short stay

	Secure unit	Hostel	O & A	Children's home	Hospital /clinic	Prison
Historical antecedents		18				
Who enters		15, 18	2, 15	2, 15, 21	15	15
Reasons for entry		18	2	2, 21		
Routes taken		18				
Goals		18	2	2, 21		
Regimes		18	2	2, 21		

Influential factors

	Secure unit	Hostel	O & A	Children's home	Hospital /clinic	Prison
Formal structure		18	2	2, 21		
Staff world		18	2	2, 21		
Child world		18	2	2, 21		
Relations with outside world		18	2	2		
Relations with family		18	2	2		
Functions for wider care system		18				

Effects and outcomes

	Secure unit	Hostel	O & A	Children's home	Hospital /clinic	Prison
while there		18		21		
on leaving		18		21		
short-term		18		21		
long-term		18				

Ordinary boarding school	EBD/ Special boarding school	CHE	Children's home	Hospital	Prison	Secure unit	Long stay
11		13		14			Historical antecedents
11, 15	10, 15, 25	2, 5, 6, 7, 13, 15, 17, 20, 23	2, 10, 15, 21	1, 14, 15	3, 15		Who enters
11, 26	10, 22, 25	2, 5, 6, 7, 13, 17, 20, 23	2, 10, 21	1, 14	3		Reasons for entry
11, 12		13			3		Routes taken
11, 12, 24, 26	10, 22, 25	2, 4, 5, 6, 9, 13, 16, 17, 19, 23	2, 10, 21	1, 14	3		Goals
11, 12, 24, 26	10, 22, 25	2, 4, 5, 6, 9, 13, 16, 17, 19, 23	2, 10, 21	1, 14	3		Regimes

Influential factors

Ordinary boarding school	EBD/ Special boarding school	CHE	Children's home	Hospital	Prison	Secure unit	
11, 12, 24, 26	10, 22, 25	2, 4, 5, 6, 9, 13, 16, 17, 19, 20, 23	2, 10, 21	1, 14	3		Formal structure
11, 12, 24, 26	10, 22, 25	2, 4, 5, 6, 9, 13, 16, 17, 19, 20, 23	2, 10, 21	1, 14	3		Staff world
11, 12, 24, 26	10, 22, 25	2, 4, 5, 6, 13, 16, 17, 19, 20, 23	2, 10, 21	1, 14	3		Child world
11, 12, 24, 26		2, 13, 17, 20, 23	2				Relations with outside world
11, 12, 26		2, 13, 17, 20, 23	2				Relations with family
		13, 23					Functions for wider care system

Effects and outcomes

Ordinary boarding school	EBD/ Special boarding school	CHE	Children's home	Hospital	Prison	Secure unit	
11, 12, 24, 26	10, 22	4, 5, 6, 13, 17, 20, 23	10, 21	1, 14	3		while there
11	10, 22	4, 5, 6, 13, 17, 20, 23	10, 21	1, 14	3		on leaving
11	10, 22	5, 6, 13, 17, 20	10, 21		3		short-term
		5, 6, 13, 17, 20					long-term

A 1 **Bartak, L.** and **Rutter, M.**
"The measurement of staff-child interaction in three units for autistic children"
An examination of the effects of different approaches to special educational treatment. pp. 171-202 in Tizard, J., Sinclair, I. and Clarke, R. (eds)
Varieties of Residential Experience

ROUTLEDGE & KEGAN PAUL, 1975

Three units with different residential approaches were compared in order to assess the educational progress made by autistic children in each regime and to determine whether educational progress was associated with social environment. Instruments were developed to measure staff-child interaction. Best scholastic progress was made in the Unit which taught specific skills, had a high staff-pupil ratio and was well controlled. Benefits for behaviour at home were fewer.

A 2 **Berry, J.**
Daily Experience in Residential Life: A Study of Children and their Care-givers
A review of daily living and routines in a variety of child-care residential placements.

ROUTLEDGE & KEGAN PAUL, 1975

A survey of 44 residential settings for children was based on evidence gathered by students on placement. Variety in the details of daily life of children and staff (e.g. washing, eating and leisure) is discussed. Frequent difficulties experienced by staff with regard to relations with children, colleagues and the external environment were examined.

A 3 **Bottoms, A.** and **McClintock, F.**
Criminals Coming of Age
A comparative study of the outcomes achieved with Borstal boys in a traditional regime and in an experimental regime which stressed the individualisation of training.

HEINEMANN, 1973

Matched groups of 250/300 boys were followed up. No obvious differences in subsequent nature and extent of criminality were uncovered; result of regime difference was therefore seen as disappointing. Models of achieving effective organisational change are proposed.

A 4 **Clarke, R.** and **Martin, D.**
Absconding From Approved Schools
An attempt to measure, compare and explain absconding from approved schools.

HOME OFFICE RESEARCH UNIT, HMSO, 1971

Absconding was examined in the light of Learning Theory. The personality of absconders, differing absconding rates between schools, and environmental variables were considered. Environmental factors were found to be important but habitual absconding was seen as a learned response.

A 5 **Cornish, D.** and **Clarke, R.**
Residential Care and its Effects on Juvenile Delinquency
An evaluation of a controlled trial in a boys' approved school.

HMSO, 1975

Boys considered suitable for a therapeutic unit were allocated randomly to two contrasting regimes – one orthodox training, the other therapeutic treatment. Follow-up studies revealed few differences in subsequent re-offending that might be attributable to the different regimes.

A 6   **Dunlop, A.**
The Approved School Experience
An assessment of boys'
experiences of training under
different regimes in approved
schools and an evaluation of the
effectiveness of that training.
HOME OFFICE RESEARCH REPORT,
HMSO, 1974

It emerged from a study of 470 boys in 9
schools that the best liked aspect of school
was work training.   Schools emphasising
this were more successful, not because of
their regime but because training led boys to
behave in ways that reduced the likelihood
of reconviction, for example by giving them
opportunities for independence and maturity.

A 7   **Gilbert, J.**
"Delinquent (approved school)
and non-delinquent (secondary
modern) girls"
A comparison of 14-16 year old
girls, 400 in approved schools
and 200 in secondary modern in
order to examine differences in
background characteristics and
factors relevant to delinquency.
pp 325-56, *British Journal of
Criminology,* XII, 1972.

There were many similarities in the girls'
background but the offenders had poor
discipline from mothers and displayed greater
anomie. Differences in the children's perception
of their parents' relationship with them and of
their economic status were also found to be
significant.

A 8   **Gill, O.**
*Whitegate: An Approved School
in Transition*
A description of change in a
boys' approved school from the
boys' point of view.
LIVERPOOL UNIVERSITY PRESS, 1974

Boys' perceptions of the functions and aims
of the school contrasted with those of the
staff.   Boys saw it as controlling their
delinquency and not meeting their welfare
needs.   Hence, they conformed in order to
get early release.

A 9   **Heal, K.** and **Cawson, P.**
"Organisation and change in
children's institutions"
A cross-institutional study to
determine how far approved
schools might achieve a
'community home' model.
pp. 69-101 in Tizard, J., Sinclair,
I., and Clarke, R. (eds)
*Varieties of Residential
Experience*
ROUTLEDGE & KEGAN PAUL, 1975

A comparative study of nine schools,
considering the organisation and environment as perceived by children and staff, and
examining staff roles and decision making.
All schools found it difficult to combine
education and therapeutic goals but some
achieved considerable change through
delegating staff responsibility, reducing
regimentation and introducing more liberal
or democratic processes.

^{A} 10 **King, R., Raynes, N. and Tizard, J.**
Patterns of Residential Care
A comparative study of units, including some children's homes, for children with handicaps.
ROUTLEDGE & KEGAN PAUL, 1971

A comparison of organisational factors and child-management practices which considered routine, block treatment, rigidity and social distance between children and staff. Local authority hostels and voluntary homes were more child-oriented than hospitals, a situation that affected children's progress.

^{A} 11 **Lambert, R., Bullock, R. and Millham, S.**
The Chance of a Lifetime? A Study of Boarding Education
A study of boarding education.
WEIDENFELD AND NICOLSON, 1975

A survey of 68 boarding schools which examined the background of the pupils, boarding styles and the effects of residence on children. Schools varied widely in approach and aims. Distinct effects were identified with respect to academic attainment, family relationships and peer relations, but so much depended on the type of boarding experienced that generalisation was difficult.

^{A} 12 **Lambert, R. and Millham, S.**
The Hothouse Society
An exploration of boarding school life through the boys' and girls' own writings.
WEIDENFELD AND NICOLSON, 1968

A collection of children's writings on school life based on a study of 86 schools and 22,700 pupils. The variety of structures was found to be wide and pupils' responses varied greatly. The relationship between formal and informal social systems was a key influence on the opinions expressed.

^{A} 13 **Millham, S., Bullock, R. and Cherrett, P.**
After Grace —Teeth
A comparative study of 18 boys' approved schools examining their intake, their stylistic variety and the after-care careers of the boys.
HUMAN CONTEXT BOOKS, 1975

A study of 18 institutions and a two year follow-up of boys after leaving. Regimes were classified into five types: Junior training, Senior training, Therapeutic, Campus and Family Group. Outcomes for boys while resident varied considerably according to regime; the effects on later delinquency were less marked. Regime differences only accounted for a 10% variation in re-offending rates, much of which was due to boys' behaviour while there. The informal worlds of the boys and the staff were studied to indentify conditions which reinforced or challenged institutional goals. In the less successful institutions, there was clear evidence of a criminal, anti-social sub-culture.

A 14 Morris, P.

Put Away: A Sociological Study of Institutions for the Mentally Retarded
A sociological study of institutions for the mentally retarded.

ROUTLEDGE & KEGAN PAUL, 1969

Twenty-four homes with 1,697 residents were the subject of a comparative study which included an analysis of population, physical environment and facilities, staffing problems, education and training resources and quality of life, and an assessment of relationships inside the hospitals and between the hospitals and the outside world. A gloomy picture emerged of isolated institutions and beleaguered staff.

A 15 Moss, P.

"Residential care of children: A general view"
A survey of the numbers and characteristics of all children in residential settings; pp. 17-51 in Tizard, J., Sinclair, I. and Clarke, R. (eds) *Varieties of Residential Experience*

ROUTLEDGE & KEGAN PAUL, 1975

Over 4,300 units were identified and the number of children living in them estimated at 235,850. Boys outnumbered girls, especially in approved schools. Big differences were found in average size, geographical spread, staffing patterns and specialisation.

A 16 Polsky, H.

Cottage Six
An investigation of the social systems created by delinquent boys in residential treatment.

SAGE FOUNDATION, 1962

From an intensive study of a cottage in a reform school it emerged that the informal culture was supportive of some institutional aims, but sufficiently powerful to undermine welfare and treatment goals.

A 17 Richardson, H.

Adolescent Girls in Approved Schools
A survey of girls in approved schools.

ROUTLEDGE & KEGAN PAUL, 1969

An examination of the personal and family characteristics, social and family backgrounds and previous welfare involvement of 550 girls. Sixty per cent were considered generally to do well after leaving and few turned out to be persistent offenders. The approved school system is described and some evidence on outcomes offered.

A 18 Sinclair, I.

Hostels for Probationers
A comparative study of 17 probation hostels and the progress of 429 boys sheltered over a one year period.

HMSO, 1971

A comparative analysis of boys' backgrounds, hostel programmes, control systems and the characteristics of wardens and staff. There is follow-up evidence on absconding and offending. Failure rates were found to vary significantly, mostly as a result of behaviour while in the hostels. Influences on success rates were associated with staff and transient factors rather than with variables associated with hostel situations.

ᴬ 19	**Sparrow, J.** *Diary of a Delinquent Episode* The autobiography of a young staff member in a girls' approved school. ROUTLEDGE & KEGAN PAUL, 1975	An intensive study of staff world and pupil culture which demonstrated how interaction between the two simultaneously generated and responded to girls' behaviour problems.
ᴬ 20	**Street, D., Vinter, R.** and **Perrow, C.** *Organisation for Treatment* A comparative study of reform schools. FREE PRESS, 1966	A comparison of six schools, two each from the point of view of an emphasis on obedience, conformity and treatment. Pupils' responses to their situation were gauged. Successful schools did not conform to any particular model but were those that delegated power to staff, had good relations with the local community, showed organisational flexibility, had good executive leadership and could adapt to change.
ᴬ 21	**Tizard, B.** "Varieties of nursery experience" An analysis of residential nursery approaches and their effects on staff and child behaviour. pp. 102-121 in Tizard, J., Sinclair, I. and Clarke, R. (eds) *Varieties of Residential* *Experience* ROUTLEDGE & KEGAN PAUL, 1975	Through comparative analysis of 13 nurseries, formal structures, especially the autonomy of sub-units, were examined. The extent to which 'mothering' was employed by staff varied. Language development depended on the amount and type of staff talk, opportunities for which were circumscribed by levels of staff autonomy. However, follow-up studies of children indicated no educational retardation when aged three to five.
ᴬ 22	**Tizard, J.** "Quality of residential care for retarded children" A comparative study of units in homes and hospitals from the point of view of organisation and child-management. pp. 52- 68 in Tizard, J., Sinclair, I., Clarke, R. (eds) *Varieties of* *Residential Experience* ROUTLEDGE & KEGAN PAUL, 1975	Very wide differences in child-management practices, staff development, staff roles and performance were identified. Generally, the more child-oriented the regime, the better children's progress in feeding and speech.
ᴬ 23	**Tutt, N.** *Care or Custody* A study of a boys' approved school. DARTON, LONGMAN & TODD, 1974	From an intensive study of boys and staff it emerged that tension and conflict existed where care and custody aims were concerned. Staff and boys adapted to achieve a *modus vivendi*.

A 24 **Wakeford, J.**
The Cloistered Elite
A sociological analysis of the English public boarding school.

MACMILLAN, 1969

A study of the school as an organisation, focussing on the roles, rituals and ranking system. Pupils' perspectives and adaptations were examined in the context of the structure described. Their responses varied between conformity, retreatism, rebellion and colonisation. They saw their experience as more depriving than staff or parents realised.

A 25 **Wills, D.**
Spare the Child
A study of change at the Cotswold Community.

PENGUIN, 1971

Through a case study of a boys' approved school, in transition from a traditional structure to a therapeutic community, changes in the attitudes of staff, boys and the local community were charted.

A 26 **Wober, M.**
English Girls' Boarding Schools
A comparative study of 23 girls' boarding schools.

ALLEN LANE, 1971

A comparison of regimes, aims and effects. Girls who coped best with the regime were those who had secure family relationships and parents who had themselves been boarders. Regimes were geared to a particular social and cultural group in society.

B

Publications since 1975

B

Publications since 1975

Numbers refer to the alphabetical listings on pages 42-49

Short stay	Secure unit	Hostel	O & A	Children's home	Hospital / clinic	Prison
Historical antecedents	9, 19		23	4, 23		
Who enters	9, 14, 19, 29	2, 20	20, 28	4, 11, 20, 28		18
Reasons for entry	9, 14, 19, 29	2, 20	20, 28	4, 11, 20, 28, 35		18
Routes taken	9, 14, 19	20	20, 28	4, 20, 28, 35		18
Goals	19, 29	2		3, 4, 11, 35		18
Regimes	19, 29	2	6	4, 11, 12, 15, 35		18

Influential factors

	Secure unit	Hostel	O & A	Children's home	Hospital / clinic	Prison
Formal structure	19, 29	2		3, 4, 11, 12, 35		18
Staff world	19	2		3, 4, 11, 12, 35		18
Child world	19	2	6	11, 12, 15, 35		18
Relations with outside world	19		6	4, 11, 12, 35		
Relations with family		20	6, 20	4, 11, 12, 20, 35		
Functions for wider care system	19	20	10, 20, 28	4, 10, 20, 28		

Effects and outcomes

	Secure unit	Hostel	O & A	Children's home	Hospital / clinic	Prison
while there	19, 29	2, 20	6, 20, 28	15, 20, 28, 35		18
on leaving	19	20	6, 20, 28	15, 20, 28, 35		18
short-term	19			15		
long-term	19					

Ordinary boarding school	EBD/ Special boarding school	CHE	Children's home	Hospital	Prison	Secure Unit	*Long stay*
		1, 23	4, 23		23	9, 16, 19	*Historical antecedents*
		1, 20, 25, 28	4, 11, 17, 20, 28	22	18, 31	9, 13, 14, 24, 29, 31	*Who enters*
		1, 20, 25, 28, 34	4, 11, 17, 20, 28, 35	22	18, 31	9, 13, 14, 24, 29, 31	*Reasons for entry*
		20, 28	4, 20, 28, 35		18, 31	9, 13, 14, 19, 31	*Routes taken*
26, 33		24, 34	3, 4, 11, 35	22	18, 31	13, 16, 18, 24, 29, 31	*Goals*
26, 33		1, 5, 30, 34	4, 11, 13, 15, 17, 30, 32, 35	22	18, 31	16, 19, 29, 31	*Regimes*

Influential factors

Ordinary boarding school	EBD/ Special boarding school	CHE	Children's home	Hospital	Prison	Secure Unit	
26, 33		1, 5, 34	3, 4, 11, 12, 17, 35	22	18	16, 19, 29	*Formal structure*
33		1, 5, 8, 34	3, 4, 11, 12, 17, 35	22	18	16, 19	*Staff world*
33		1, 5, 34	11, 12, 15, 17, 35	22	18	16, 18	*Child world*
33		7	4, 7, 11, 12, 17, 35	22		19	*Relations with outside world*
		20, 25	4, 11, 12, 17, 20, 35				*Relations with family*
		10, 20	4, 10, 20		31	13, 20, 31	*Functions of wider care system*

Effects and outcomes

Ordinary boarding school	EBD/ Special boarding school	CHE	Children's home	Hospital	Prison	Secure Unit	
26		1, 5, 20, 25, 28, 30, 34	15, 17, 20, 27, 28, 30, 35	22	18	13, 19, 24, 29	*while there*
26		20, 25, 28, 30	15, 17, 20, 27, 28, 30, 35	22	18	13, 19, 24	*on leaving*
26		25, 30	15, 17, 25, 27, 30, 32	22		13, 19, 24	*short-term*
26		25	27, 32			13, 19, 24	*long-term*

No.	Author and Subject	Methods and Findings

B 1 **Ackland, J.**
Girls in Care
A case study of CHE with an analysis of organisation, staff and girls' perceptions, control, discipline and institutional reactions.
GOWER, 1982

It emerged that ideas concerning care and treatment were difficult to implement. Treatment was a response measured more to the girls' behaviour than to their needs, and they saw the CHE as punitive. Bad behaviour served other functions, such as to make possible an escape from group living. Homeless, institutionalised girls had little incentive to behave. Thus, staff perceptions of girls' problems exacerbated an already difficult situation.

B 2 **Andrews, J.**
Hostels for Offenders
A survey of hostels for offenders.
HMSO, 1979

A variety of structures, administration and aims of hostels for offenders was charted.

B 3 **Baldwin, N.**
The Power to Care in Children's Homes
An explanation of why staff in community homes find it difficult to achieve high standards of care.
AVEBURY, 1990

An analysis of the writer's consultancy work with staff groups in community homes. Staff difficulties stemmed from feelings of powerlessness, remote decision-making, isolation, the residual functions of residential care, and from the perception that the children were the authors of their own misfortunes.

B 4 **Berridge, D.**
Children's Homes
A survey of 20 children's homes.
BLACKWELL, 1985

A comparative study of residential children's homes examining the backgrounds of children and staff, regimes and approaches to particular problems, such as education and relations with families. Homes were found to have important but varied functions for care systems (e.g. reception, crisis, preparation for foster care) and to vary in style.

B 5 **Bramham, P.**
How Staff Rule
A study of ways in which staff in two boys' CHEs exercised control.
SAXON HOUSE, 1980

The informal worlds of staff and boys and the relationship between them were studied. It emerged that effective control depended on a complex process of negotiation, social consensus and structural power.

B 6   **Bullock, R., Little, M.** and
Millham, S.
Going Home: The Return of
Children Separated from their
Families
A study of children's return home
after absence in care. The
process of reunion was analysed
in the light of findings from a
longitudinal study of returning
children. The focus included
return from residential care.

DARTMOUTH, 1993

See also: Bullock, R., Hosie, K.,
Little, M. and Millham, S., "The
problems of managing the family
contacts of children in residential
care". pp. 591-610, *British Journal*
of Social Work, XX, 1990

Return was shown to be every bit as stressful
as separation and frequently subject to
breakdown. It was demonstrated that,
contrary to common belief, nine out of ten
children in care were eventually re-united
with their families. Key findings were
incorporated in Checklists which help predict
the likelihood and success of return.

B 7   **Burgess, C.**
In Care and into Work
A study of leavers from a boys'
CHE making the transition from
care to work.

TAVISTOCK, 1981

Care problems and poor qualifications
compounded the difficulties associated with
leaving. In the move to work and independent
living, the benefits of residential care tended
to be overwhelmed by the wider problems
young people faced.

B 8   **Cawson, P.**
Community Homes:
A Study of Residential Staff
A study of staff roles, attitudes
and job satisfaction in 3 CHEs.

HMSO, 1978

Data on staff and evaluation of their roles
and job situation were considered in the
light of changes in child-care philosophy.
Key issues identified were delegation of
powers, the role of heads and integrating
education and care staff.

B 9   **Cawson, P.** and **Martell, M.**
Children Referred to Closed
Units
A study of all referrals to closed
units over a two year period.

HMSO, 1979

Children's backgrounds, previous care
histories and presenting problems were
analysed and the data reviewed in the light
of policy questions on the need for secure
units. Referrals were not identified as the
most pressing cases; factors such as the
availability of beds and rejection by other
systems, were often found to be important.
Demands for security were fuelled by
pressures other than the severity of children's
presenting problems.

B 10 Cliffe, D. and **Berridge, D.**
Closing Children's Homes
An evaluation of Warwickshire
SSD's policy of not providing
residential child-care facilities.

NATIONAL CHILDREN'S BUREAU, 1992

All likely candidates for residential care in Warwickshire were surveyed and follow-up studies made of their placements. Since the county's policy was an evolutionary one, alternative foster care had long been an option. Outcomes for those fostered were considered to be as good as or better than for those in residential care, but there were still many problems. For very difficult cases some residential care was purchased from a local voluntary agency.

B 11 Colton, M.
*Dimensions of Substitute
Child Care*
A comparison of foster and
residential care practices.

AVEBURY, 1988

Foster and residential situations were studied, particularly with regard to the management of children, children's community contacts, the provision of physical amenities, control methods and the roles and behaviour of care givers. Foster homes were found to be more child-orientated than children's homes and to cope equally well with difficult behaviour. The differences were not explained by the children's background factors.

B 12 Dharamsi, F., et al.
*Caring for Children: A Diary of a
Local Authority Children's Home*
A day-to-day account of life in a
children's home.

OWEN WELLS, 1979.

An examination of staff roles, young people's lifestyles, aspirations and interests.

**B 13 Dartington Social
Research Unit**
*The Characteristics of Young
People in Youth Treatment
Centres, 1989; Alternative Care
Careers: The Experience of Very
Difficult Adolescents Outside
Youth Treatment Centre
Provision, 1989; The Experiences
and Care Careers of Young
People Leaving Youth Treatment
Centres, 1989; The Experience of
YTC Look-alikes Sheltered in
Other Secure Settings, 1991.*
A study of the care careers and
experiences after leaving of 200
young people in YTCs.
D S R U

The backgrounds of the children showed a range of presenting problems and care careers. They included one-off grave offenders, long-term social services cases, long-term education cases and those whose problems escalated in adolescence. Follow-up studies revealed chronic problems of adjustment and re-offending for boys. Patterns of living situations were also varied. Girls generally did better than boys and Section 53 cases better than care cases. The worst outcomes were among boys who had been long in care.

B 14 **Harris, R.** and **Timms, N.** *Between Hospital and Prison or Thereabouts* A Report of a Study of the Introduction and Implementation of the Child Care Act 1980, Section 21A, and the Secure Accommodation (No.2) Regulations. Also a literature review, a policy study in 50 local authorities, a criteria study of 399 children subject to a secure accommodation order in 11 local authorities, and a scrutiny of 37 judicial hearings in 5 juvenile courts. UNIVERSITY OF LEICESTER RESEARCH REPORT TO DHSS, 1988	Interpretation of secure accommodation legislation was found to vary across England and Wales. Use of security reflected local authority policies more than central government edict. There was a lack of clarity and purpose about the function of secure units. The juvenile courts remained 'fairly toothless watchdogs'; social workers retained considerable power.
B 15 **Kahan, B.** *Growing Up in Care* Case studies of ten children growing up in care. BLACKWELL, 1979	Children's views on residential care were mixed. Individual care was possible but continuity was often disrupted by staff leaving and the provision was hampered by poor staff organisation. Issues connected with privacy, respect and courtesy, which were important to the children, were often overlooked.
B 16 **Kelly, B.** *Children Inside: Rhetoric and Practice in a Locked Institution for Children* A case study of a secure unit. ROUTLEDGE, 1992	Analysis of the relationship between the reason for children's entry, staff values and residents' perceptions. Conflicts and contrasts were explained in light of evidence that rhetoric was often at odds with actual practice.
B 17 **Lasson, I.** *Where's My Mum?* A study of the family contacts of children in long-stay children's homes. PEPAR, 1978	Children's family contacts were analysed over time. It was found that there was an inherent tendency for links to wither but that on several criteria the children in regular contact with relatives were more likely to be better adjusted.
B 18 **Little, M.** *Young Men in Prison* An examination of the criminal identity of young men in prison custody. DARTMOUTH, 1990	The study focussed on 231 young men convicted or on remand. The development of criminal identity was explained through inmate rules of behaviour. Changing identity was analysed in the context of different stages in the prison career.

B 19 **Millham, S., Bullock, R.**
and Hosie, K.
Learning to Care
An assessment of staff training
for residential social work with
children.

GOWER, 1980

A study of students training for residential
work. Student backgrounds revealed a long
history of marginality which might affect
their work performance. Their problems
with regard to taking up residential work
were related to residential tasks, the values
imbibed on courses and the backgrounds of
staff.

B 20 **Millham, S., Bullock, R.**
and Hosie, K.
Locking Up Children
A study of child-care secure
accommodation and the
provision for young offenders in
prison.

SAXON HOUSE, 1978

Children admitted were found to be difficult
but also to be casualties of the care system.
Unit styles varied but child-centred work
was possible in some unpromising situations.
Follow-up studies revealed high rates of re-
offending for boys. Detailed studies were
made of presenting problems – absconding,
violence and grave offending – and of under
18s in Borstal.

B 21 **Millham, S., Bullock, R.,**
Hosie, K. and Haak, M.
Lost in Care
A study of the problems of
maintaining links between
children in care and their
families.

GOWER, 1986

A two year follow-up study of 450 children
entering care. Residential care was found to
be used frequently, especially for adolescents
and before or after fostering. Residential
placements were used at various moments in
children's care careers, (e.g. on reception or
after first breakdown). Serious difficulties
in maintaining the family links of children
in residential care were identified.

B 22 **Oswin, M.**
Children Living
in Long-Stay Hospitals
A study of 223 profoundly
retarded children living in long-
stay hospitals.
SPASTICS INTERNATIONAL MEDICAL
PUBLICATION, 1978

see also: *The Empty Hours: A*
Study of Weekend Life of Handi-
capped Children in Institutions
PENGUIN, 1971

The hospital provision was compared, as
were the roles and tasks of staff. Nurses
were found to be dissatisfied with services
and the absence of a child-care policy on the
wards. Staff training needed improvement,
and reinforcement by changes in formal
structures and institutional philosophies.

B 23 **Parker, R.**
A History of Child-Care
A history of child-care from the
19th Century to the present day.

BARNARDOS, 1990

An analysis of the growth and contribution
of residential care. The changing administrative responsibilities and the wider social
factors that affect residential services are
discussed.

B 24 Petrie, C.
The Nowhere Boys
A comparative study of open
and closed residential
placements.

SAXON HOUSE, 1980

Two groups of 100 boys in open and closed
settings in Scotland were compared. Family
histories, placements and offending patterns
were contrasted. Some mentally handicapped
boys were found to end up in security; others
were casualties of the welfare system. Follow-
up evidence showed chronic problems to do
with employment, education and offending.

B 25 Petrie, C.
The Nowhere Girls
A comparison of boys and girls
in a Scottish List-D school.

GOWER, 1986

A study of 80 girls and 100 boys examined
family backgrounds, intelligence, school
records and histories of abuse. Girls were
far less delinquent than boys but more in
need of protection.

B 26 Punch, M.
The Progressive Retreat
A follow-up study of 25 leavers
from Dartington Hall School.

CAMBRIDGE UNIVERSITY PRESS, 1977

Close correspondence was found between
the lifestyles of young people and school
culture. The differences extended to political
attitudes, taste and relationships. Distinct
lifestyles were pursued well into adult life.

B 27 Quinton, D. and Rutter, M.
Parenting Breakdown
An examination of intra and
inter-generational continuities in
social functioning.

AVEBURY, 1988

A study of 94 women who lived in two
cottage homes in 1964 followed up to the
present day. Some continuities were identified, especially when problem cases were
examined retrospectively. Fewer emerged
from prospective evidence. Opportunities
to break such continuities are discussed.

**B 28 Rowe, J., Hundleby, M.
and Garnett, L.**
Child-Care Now
A survey of all placements
experienced by children in care
in six local authorities over a
two year period.

BRITISH AGENCIES FOR
ADOPTION AND FOSTERING, 1989

Residential care was found to be commonly
used, especially for adolescents but also in a
quarter of placements involving younger
children. Aims of residential care were very
wide; 46% of residential placements were
deemed successful and 16% unsuccessful in
terms of achieving aims and lasting as long
as required.

B 29 Staffordshire CC
*The Pindown Experience
and the Protection of Children*
An inquiry into the treatment of
children in residential care in
Staffordshire.

STAFFORDSHIRE CC, 1991

A case study of how the management of
residential services can break down and
pseudo-theories of treatment can become
ingrained. The process by which staff values
and practices develop and are maintained
was analysed. Data were assembled
concerning difficult adolescents who were
the responsibility of social services.

B 30	**Stein, M.** and **Carey, C.** *Leaving Care* An examination of the problems faced when leaving care. BLACKWELL, 1976	Interviews with young people leaving care, many from residential settings, uncovered problems of loneliness, debt and stigma and a tendency to move quickly to other group living situations or relationships.
B 31	**Stewart, G.** and **Tutt, N.** *Children in Custody* A survey of young people aged 14-16 in custody of all kinds in the United Kingdom and Eire, completed on a single day in September 1984. AVEBURY, 1987	The placements and length of stay of 1,375 young people were analysed. Rates varied by administrative sector in the different countries and in different parts of England. Length of stay varied as a core of long-stay cases was supplemented by a high turnover of short-stay cases. Penal establishments were important, providing 85% of the custody for the 14-16 year olds despite their needs for treatment and welfare.
B 32	**Triseliotis, J.** and **Russell, J.** *Hard to Place* An assessment of the outcomes of adoption and residential care. HEINEMANN, 1984	A follow-up study of 91 adoptees and 68 ex-residential placements. The residential group did better educationally but worse in every other respect. Particular problems faced were loss of contact with family, continuities, stigma and lack of care.
B 33	**Walford, G.** *Life in Public Schools* A study of two boys' schools. METHUEN, 1986	A survey of regimes, staff, curriculum and co-education. Major changes introduced in the last 20 years are discussed.
B 34	**Walter, J.** *Sent Away* A study of a boys' approved school. SAXON HOUSE, 1977	The boys' informal worlds were studied. The contrast between their views and the aims of care and treatment created tension for staff.
B 35	**Whitaker, D., Cook, J., Dunn, C.** and **Lunn-Rockliffe, S.,** *The Experience of Residential Care from the Perspective of Children, Parents and Caregivers.* The perspectives of children, parents and carers explored. UNIVERSITY OF YORK, 1984	An intensive study of residential homes, analysing and contrasting the perspectives of participants, parents, children and caregivers. Data were analysed in the context of wider psychological theories and children's continuities of experiences. Outcomes varied; children in each situation experienced gains and losses.

C

Influential Texts Cited

C

Influential texts cited

Numbers refer to the alphabetical listings on pages 52-59

Short stay

	Secure unit	Hostel	O & A	Children's home	Hospital / clinic	Prison
Historical antecedents	9		15, 24, 41	15, 24, 26, 41	5	41
Who enters			41, 49	41, 49	5, 49	41
Reasons for entry		16	7, 16, 49	16, 49	5, 49	
Routes taken						
Goals	18, 46	16, 18	2,7, 16, 18, 39, 44, 46, 49, 53, 55, 56	2, 16, 18, 26, 39, 44, 46, 49, 53, 55, 56	5, 25, 48, 49	
Regimes	18, 38, 46	18, 38	2, 7, 10, 18, 38, 40, 43, 44, 46, 49, 50, 53	2, 10, 11, 18, 38, 40, 43, 44, 46, 49, 50, 53	5, 25, 48, 49	

Influential factors

	Secure unit	Hostel	O & A	Children's home	Hospital / clinic	Prison
Formal structure	9, 18, 21, 38, 46, 47	16, 18, 21, 38, 47	2, 7, 16, 18, 21, 38, 40, 44, 46, 47, 49, 50, 53	2, 16, 18, 21, 38, 40, 44, 46, 47, 49, 50, 53	5, 21, 25, 37, 47, 48, 49	21, 47
Staff world	18, 46	17, 29	2, 7, 17, 29, 40, 44, 46, 49, 50	2, 17, 29, 40, 44, 46, 49, 50	5, 25, 37, 49	
Child world			2, 7, 44, 49, 50	2, 44, 49, 50	25, 49	
Relations with outside world	18	18	2, 7, 11, 18, 34	2, 11, 18, 34	25	
Relations with family	18, 36	18	2, 7, 18, 22, 36	2, 18, 22, 36	25	
Functions for wider care system	18	18	2, 15, 18, 22, 24, 39, 41, 43, 49	2, 15, 18, 22, 24, 26, 39, 41, 43, 49	25, 49	

Effects and outcomes

	Secure unit	Hostel	O & A	Children's home	Hospital / clinic	Prison
while there	42, 46	42	2, 19, 22, 40, 41, 42, 46, 49, 50	19, 22, 40, 41, 42, 46, 49, 50	5, 25, 37, 48, 49	
on leaving	42, 46	42	2, 19, 22, 41, 42, 49	2, 19, 22, 41, 42, 49	5, 48, 49	
short-term			2, 19, 41	2, 19, 41	5	
long-term			19, 41	19, 41		

Ordinary boarding school	EBD/Special boarding school	CHE	Children's home	Hospital	Prison	Secure Unit	Long stay
4, 30, 41	3, 12, 15, 24, 26, 30, 41	3, 14, 15, 24, 26, 30, 41	15, 24, 26, 30, 41	5	30, 41	9	Historical antecedents
41	41, 49	41, 49	41, 49	5, 49	41		Who enters
	8, 20, 27, 32, 49	7, 16, 20, 27, 49	7, 16, 27, 49	5, 49		27	Reasons for entry
	8						Routes taken
30, 31, 33, 55, 56	3, 8, 12, 18, 20, 26, 27, 30, 31, 32, 35, 39, 44, 46, 49, 53, 54, 55, 56	1, 2, 7, 14, 16, 18, 20, 26, 27, 30, 32, 35, 39, 44, 46, 49, 53, 54, 55, 56	2, 7, 16, 18, 26, 27, 30, 39, 44, 46, 49, 53, 55, 56	5, 23, 25, 48, 49	30	18, 27, 46	Goals
18, 31, 38	3, 8, 13, 18, 20, 21, 27, 31, 32, 33, 38, 40, 43, 44, 46, 49, 50, 53, 54	1, 2, 7, 13, 18, 20, 27, 32, 35, 38, 40, 43, 44, 46, 49, 50, 53, 54	2, 7, 10, 11, 18, 27, 38, 40, 43, 44, 46, 49, 50, 53, 54	5, 23, 25, 48, 49, 52		18, 27, 38, 46	Regimes

Influential factors

Ordinary boarding school	EBD/Special boarding school	CHE	Children's home	Hospital	Prison	Secure Unit	
18, 21, 31, 33, 38, 47	3, 8, 13, 18, 20, 21, 31, 32, 35, 38, 40, 44, 46, 47, 49, 50, 53, 54	1, 2, 7, 13, 14, 16, 18, 20, 23, 28, 32, 35, 38, 40, 44, 46, 47, 49, 50, 53, 54	2, 7, 16, 18, 21, 38, 40, 44, 46, 47, 49, 50, 53, 54	5, 21, 23, 25, 37, 47, 48, 49, 52	21, 47	9, 18, 21, 38, 46, 47	Formal structure
31, 33	3, 8, 17, 20, 31, 32, 40, 44, 46, 49, 50	2, 3, 7, 17, 20, 28, 29, 40, 44, 46, 49, 50, 54	2, 7, 17, 29, 40, 44, 46, 49, 50, 54	5, 23, 25, 37, 49, 52		18, 46	Staff world
31, 33	3, 8, 20, 31, 32, 44, 49, 50	2, 3, 7, 20, 28, 32, 44, 49, 50	2, 7, 44, 49, 50	23, 25, 49, 52			Child world
33	3, 11, 18, 27, 34, 54	1, 2, 3, 7, 11, 18, 27, 34, 54	2, 7, 11, 18, 27, 34, 54	23, 25		18, 27	Relations with outside world
33	3, 18, 22, 27, 36	1, 2, 7, 18, 22, 27, 36	2, 7, 18, 22, 27, 36	6, 23, 25		18, 27	Relations with family
33	15, 18, 22, 24, 26, 39, 41, 43, 49	2, 15, 18, 22, 24, 26, 39, 41, 43, 49	2, 15, 18, 22, 24, 26, 39, 41, 43, 49	6, 23, 25, 49		18	Functions for wider care system

Effects and outcomes

Ordinary boarding school	EBD/Special boarding school	CHE	Children's home	Hospital	Prison	Secure Unit	
31	3, 8, 13, 19, 22, 27, 31, 32, 35, 40, 41, 42, 46, 49, 50	2, 13, 19, 22, 27, 28, 32, 35, 40, 41, 42, 46, 49, 50	2, 19, 22, 27, 40, 41, 42, 46, 49, 50	5, 6, 23, 25, 37, 48, 49, 52		27, 42, 46	while there
31	3, 8, 19, 22, 27, 31, 32, 41, 42, 46, 49	2, 19, 22, 27, 32, 41, 42, 46, 49	2, 19, 22, 27, 41, 42, 46, 49	5, 6, 23, 48, 49, 52		27, 42, 46	on leaving
	3, 8, 19, 27, 41	2, 19, 27, 41	2, 19, 27, 41	5, 6, 23, 52		27	short-term
	19, 27, 41	19, 27, 41	19, 27, 41	6, 23		27	long-term

<table>
<tr><td>C 8</td><td>Bettleheim, B. (cont'd.)
Truants From Life: The Rehabilitation of Emotionally Disturbed Children
COLLIER-MACMILLAN, 1955

The Empty Fortress
FREE PRESS 1967

A Home for the Heart
ALFRED A. KNOPF, 1974</td><td></td></tr>
<tr><td>C 9</td><td>Blumenthal, G. D.
Development of Secure Units in Child Care
GOWER, 1985</td><td>A history of the development of secure units. Discussion of the functioning of secure accommodation. Analysis of the building and design of units in the United Kingdom.</td></tr>
<tr><td>C 10</td><td>Brearley, P., Hall, F., Gutridge, P., Jones, G. and Roberts, G.,
Admission to Residential Care
TAVISTOCK, 1980</td><td>A general discussion of admission to residential care, especially the legal aspects of entry. Special chapter on admission as it affects children.</td></tr>
<tr><td>C 11</td><td>Brearley, P., Black, J., Gutridge, P., Roberts, G. and Tarran, G.
Leaving Residential Care
TAVISTOCK, 1982</td><td>A general discussion of leaving residential care. Special chapter on leaving as it affects children.</td></tr>
<tr><td>C 12</td><td>Bridgeland, M. and McCann, W.
Pioneer Work with Maladjusted Children
STAPLES PRESS, 1971</td><td>A study of pioneers of work with maladjusted children and a comparison of their values and methods.</td></tr>
<tr><td>C 13</td><td>Brown, B. and Christie, M.
Social Learning Practice in Residential Child Care
PERGAMON, 1981</td><td>An introduction to social learning practice. Case study of the Gilbey Unit. Assessment of staff training needs for this type of work.</td></tr>
<tr><td>C 14</td><td>Carlebach, J.
Caring for Troubled Children
ROUTLEDGE & KEGAN PAUL, 1970</td><td>A history of approved schools and a review of the situation then current. Special focus on the role of school managers.</td></tr>
</table>

C 15 Davis, A.
The Residential Solution:
State Alternatives to Family Care
TAVISTOCK, 1981

A discussion of the role of residential care in Britain. Present policies analysed in their historical context. Family substitute care is distinguished from family-alternative care and family-supplement care.

C 16 Department of Health
Children in Public Care
The Utting Report
HMSO, 1991.

for Welsh and Scottish focus
Accommodating Children
WELSH OFFICE, 1992
and

Skinner, A.
Another Kind of Home
HMSO, 1992

A review of the condition of residential child-care looking particularly at management, regimes, staff and children's rights. Appropriate controls have been identified in the 1993 Local Authority Circular No. LAC (93)13: **Department of Health**, *Guidance on permissible forms of control in children's residential care.*

C 17 Department of Health
Choosing with Care
(The Warner Report)
HMSO, 1992

The report of a committee examining the selection of staff for residential work and related management issues.

C 18 Department of Health
Residential Care
Vol. 4 of the 1989 *Children Act*
Guidance and Regulations
HMSO, 1991

see also: *Independent Schools*,
Vol. 5

and, *The Welfare of Children in Boarding Schools*
HMSO, 1991

Regulations concerning the residential provision for children placed under the 1989 *Children Act*.

C 19 Dinnage, R. R. and **Pringle, K.**
Residential Child-Care: Facts and Fallacies
LONGMAN, 1967

A comprehensive review of research findings on residential child-care up to 1966

C 20 Docker-Drysdale, B.
Papers on Residential Work:
Therapy in Child-Care
LONGMAN, 1968.

A discussion of therapy methods for working with disturbed children. Model of personality, need and treatment proposed.

C 21 Etzioni, A.
Complex Organisations
FREE PRESS, 1961

A model of organisational structure which relates goals, controls and staff and client adaptations by developing the concept of compliance.

C 22 **Fanshel, D.** and **Shinn, E.**
Children in Foster Care
COLUMBIA UNIVERSITY PRESS, 1977

A longitudinal study of children in various types of care settings, including residential homes, relationships scrutinised between children absent in care and their familes.

C 23 **Goffman, E.**
Asylums
DOUBLEDAY, 1961

A study of total institutions and the ways they control their residents. Staff and inmate adaptations considered.

C 24 **Gottesman, M.**
Residential Care: An International Reader
WHITING AND BIRCH, 1991

A collection of papers from Europe (including Central and Eastern Europe), Israel and North America describing the system of residential care and education in various countries.

C 25 **Hall, D.** and **Stacey, M.** (eds)
Beyond Separation
ROUTLEDGE & KEGAN PAUL, 1979

A study of children in hospital and of ways of coping with separation. The importance of sociological factors is stressed and their relationship to psychological variables explored.

C 26 **Hellinckx, W., Broekaert, E., Vanden Berge, A.** and **Colton, M.** (eds)
Innovations in Residential Care
ACCO 1991
see also: Van der Ploeg, J., Van der Bergh, P., Klomp, M., Knorth, E. and Smit, M. (eds) *Vulnerable Youth in Residential Care*
GARANT, 1992

Papers from international seminars on residential care describing research findings from several European countries and from North America.

C 27 **Hoghughi, M.**
Treating Problem Children
SAGE, 1988.
see also:*Troubled and Troublesome: Coping with Severely Disturbed Children*
BURNETT/ANDRE DEUTSCH, 1978

A discussion of the range of treatment options and the circumstances in which each is appropriate. Physical, behavioural, cognitive, talking, group and environmental therapies are described. Based on work at Aycliffe.

C 28 **Home Office**
Disturbances at Carlton School
HOME OFFICE, 1959.

An inquiry into disturbances at Carlton Approved School.

C 29 **Howe, E.**
The Quality of Care
(The Howe Report)
LOCAL GOVERNMENT
MANAGEMENT BOARD, 1992

A Report of the Residential Staff Inquiry, which looked at the pay and employment conditions of residential care workers.

C 30 **Jones, K.** and **Fowles, A.**
Ideas on Institutions
ROUTLEDGE & KEGAN PAUL, 1984

A discussion of historical aspects of institutional care in Britain and USA. Philosophies and research findings as they apply to particular types of service are described.

C 31 **Kashti, Y.**
The Socializing Community: Disadvantaged Adolescents in Israeli Youth Villages
and (with Arieli, M.)
Residential Settings: Socialization in Powerful Environments
DAGA, 1976

People in Institutions: The Israeli Scene
FREUND, 1986

Residential Settings and the Community: Congruence and Conflict
FREUND, 1987

A discussion of residential schools and homes in Israel with particular reference to the functions for society, the socializing effects on residents, and tensions in relations with children's families and with the wider community.

see also:
Arieli, M., Kashti, Y. and Schlasky, S.
Living at School: Israeli Residential Schools as People-Processing Organizations
RAMOT, 1983

C 32 **Konopka, G.**
Therapeutic Group Work with Children
UNIVERSITY OF MINNEAPOLIS PRESS, 1946

Group Work in the Institution
ASSOCIATED PRESS, 1954

A discussion of the therapeutic work with children in residential settings. The author has a special interest in the needs of girls

see also: *Adolescent Girls in Conflict*
PRENTICE HALL, 1966).

C 33 **Lambert, R., Millham, S.** and **Bullock, R.**
A Manual to the Sociology of the School
WEIDENFELD AND NICOLSON, 1970

A framework and methodology for studying and comparing residential schools.

C 34 **Ligthart, L.**
Community Care Inside and Outside Residential Settings
F I C E, 1987

A discussion of the relationships between community care and residential approaches.

C 35   Lyman R., Prentice-Dunn, S. and **Gabel, S.** (eds) *Residential Treatment of Children and Adolescents* PLENUM, 1989

A review of the issues and problems associated with residential treatment of young people, and a discussion of appropriate models.

C 36   Maluccio, A., Fein, E., Hamilton, J., Sutton, M. and Ward, D. "Permanency Planning and Residential Child-Care." pp. 92-107 in *Child Care Quarterly*, XI, 1982

The implications of the concept of permanency planning in residential work with children.

see also: Maluccio, A. and Whittaker, J. in Ninnally E. et al. (eds) *Troubled Relationships*, Sage, 1988, on the relationship between children's families and residential establishments.

C 37   Menzies, I. *The Functioning of Social Systems as a Defence Against Anxiety* TAVISTOCK INSTITUTE OF HUMAN RELATIONS, 1970

and

Menzies Lyth, I. *Containing Anxiety In Institutions: Selected Essays* FREE ASSOCIATION BOOKS, 1985

Discussion of the ways staff resolve problems associated with caring for difficult and disturbed young people. Emphasis on defence mechanisms which may reduce anxiety and stress but can adversely affect the quality of care.

C 38   Millham, S., Bullock, R., Hosie, K. and Haak, M. *Issues of Control in Residential Child-Care* HMSO, 1981

A review of research perspectives and knowledge with regard to control in residential child-care. Application of conclusions to various types of child-care provision in Britain. Discussion of control in the wider context of institutional aims and methods.

C 39   National Institute for Social Work *Residential Care: A Positive Choice and The Research Reviewed (The Wagner Report)* HMSO 1980

A review of all aspects of residential care and a comprehensive review of research available, with a chapter on the provision for children.

C 40   NSPCC *Institutional Abuse of Children* NSPCC, 1991

Discussion of types of institutional abuse. Analysis of the ways of protecting children in residential care. Implications of abuse risks for staff and institutional effectiveness.

C 41   **Parker, R.**
        "An historical background" and
        "Client review: Children" in
        *Residential Care: The Research
        Reviewed*
        NISW, 1988

History of residential child-care in Britain.
Review of numbers and statistical trends in
different types of care. Discussion of the
functions of residential care for the wider
welfare system. Analysis of care objectives
for children with different needs. Conclusions
on the effects of residential child-care.

C 42   **Parker, R., Ward, H., Jackson,
        S., Aldgate, J.** and **Wedge, P.**
        *Looking After Children:
        Assessing Outcomes
        in Child-Care*
        HMSO, 1991

A framework and methodology for assessing
the outcomes for children, families and
social services departments of child-care
policy and practice.

C 43   **Payne, C.** and **White, K.** (eds)
        *Caring for Deprived Children:
        International Case Studies of
        Residential Settings*
        CROOM HELM, 1979

A collection of papers on residential settings
in different countries.

C 44   **Polsky, H.** and **Claster, D.**
        *The Dynamics of Residential
        Treatment*
        UNIVERSITY OF NORTH CAROLINA
        PRESS, 1968

A model of staff-child interactions and the
informal staff and child worlds in residential
treatment units. Developed from the authors'
research studies.

C 45   **Rose, M.**
        Healing Hurt Minds
        TAVISTOCK/ROUTLEDGE 1990

A discussion and analysis of therapeutic
communities for adolescents.

C 46   **Schaefer, C.** and **Swanson, A.**
        *Children in Residential Care:
        Critical Issues in Treatment*
        VAN NOSTRAND REINHOLD, 1988

A discussion of future trends in residential
treatment for children. Review of clinical
issues to do with separation, loss, sexual
acting-out, emotional, peer culture and family
work. Review of management issues relating
to staff training, directors' influence, quality
assurance and institutional abuse.

C 47   **Silverman, D.**
        The Theory of Organisations
        HEINEMANN, 1970

A theoretical model for analysing residential
organisations.

C 48   **Steinberg, D.** (ed)
        The Adolescent Unit
        JOHN WILEY AND SONS, 1986

A collection of papers concerning an
adolescent psychiatric unit. Issues discussed
include opportunities for therapy, the
curriculum, staff roles and tasks and future
developments.

No.	Author and Subject	Focus